This Ladybird book belongs to

_____

Published by Ladybird Books Ltd
27 Wrights Lane London W8 5TZ
A Penguin Company
© LADYBIRD BOOKS LTD MCMXCIX
LADYBIRD and the device of a Ladybird are trademarks of Ladybird Books Ltd

I'm learning about...
colours
and shapes

illustrated by SUE KING

Ladybird

Red

Fox is painting something red.

What is Fox painting?

There are lots of different reds.

Rosy red

fiery red

pinky red

cherry red

Can you name these red things?

Can you think of any more?

Blue

Bluebird is painting something blue.

There are lots of different blues.

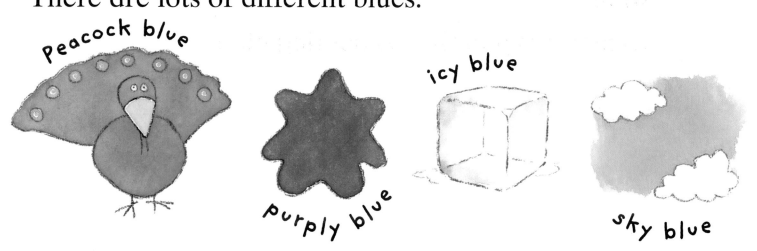

Peacock blue

purply blue

icy blue

sky blue

Can you name these blue things?

Can you think of any more?

Yellow

Lion is painting something yellow.

What is Lion painting?

There are lots of different yellows.

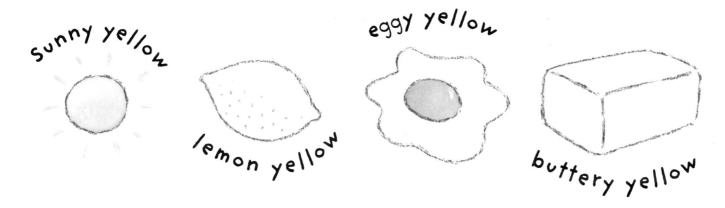

Sunny yellow

eggy yellow

lemon yellow

buttery yellow

Can you name these yellow things?

Can you think of any more?

Green

Bluebird and Lion are painting something green.
Bluebird is using blue and Lion is using yellow.

Blue and yellow mixed together make green.

There are lots of different greens.

Grass green

sea green

pine green

pea green

Can you name these green things?

Can you think of any more?

Orange

Fox and Lion are painting something orange.

Fox is using red and Lion is using yellow.

Red and yellow mixed together make orange.

What are Fox and Lion painting?

There are lots of different shades of orange.

Peachy orange

pumpkin orange

pale orange

flame orange

Can you name these orange things?

Can you think of any more?

Purple

Bluebird and Fox are painting something purple.
Bluebird is using blue and Fox is using red.

Blue and red mixed together make purple.

What are Bluebird and Fox painting?

There are lots of different purples.

Pale purple

midnight purple

lilac purple

pinky purple

Can you name these purple things?

Can you think of any more?

Black and white

All these animals are black and white.

Black and white together can make lots of different things. They can make…

stripes

spots

checks

music

printing

bear

writing

Shopping List
cakes
chocolate
cat food

Can you think of any more?

Circle

One curved edge that goes
all the way round…

There is one long, round edge.

There are no corners.

What's this shape?

It's a CIRCLE!

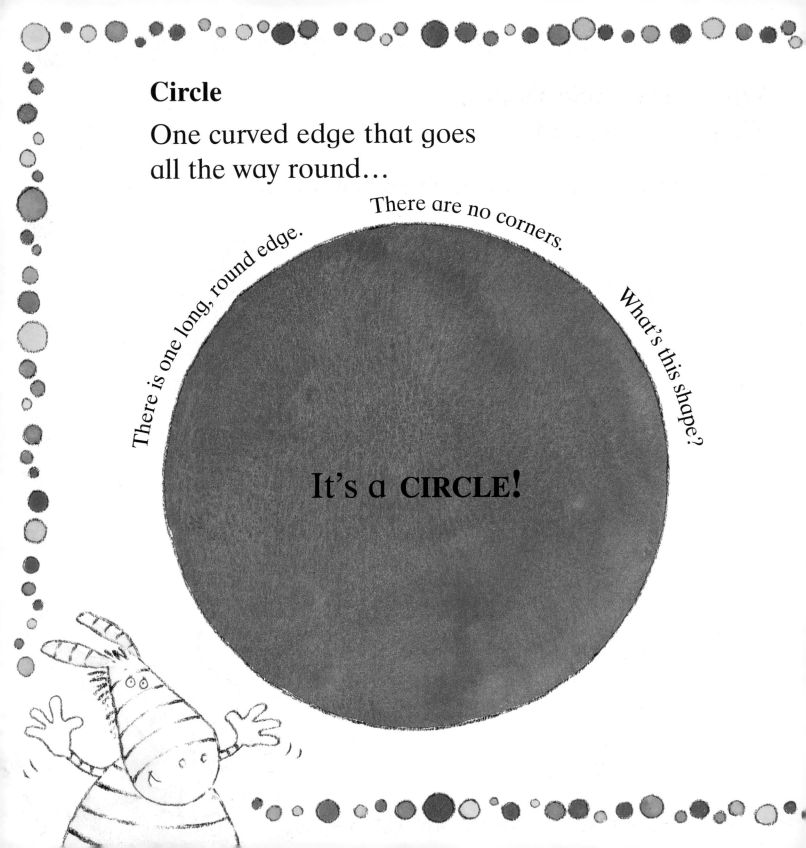

Wheels are circle shapes.
They go round and round.

How many wheels does each vehicle have?

Which would
you like
to drive?

Square

Four straight sides,
one, two, three, four…

There are four sides.

There are four corners.

All four sides are the same.

It's a **SQUARE!**

What's this shape?

The windows on these houses are square shapes.
Some are big and some are small.

Can you count the windows on each house?

Find my
house. It has
three windows.

Triangle

Three sides, three corners,
one, two, three…

There are three sides.

It's a **TRIANGLE!**

There are three corners.

What's this shape?

Can you trace round the triangle?

These party hats are triangle shapes.
They are different sizes but they are all triangles.

What shape are Panda's pockets?

Which hat do you like best?

Rectangle

Two sides are long,
two sides are short,
one, two, three, four…

There are four sides. This side is long.

There are four corners.

This side is short.

It's a **RECTANGLE!**

What's this shape?

Follow the edges with your finger.

These doors and drawers are rectangles.
Some are short and some are long.

How many rectangles can you count?

Who's behind the blue door?

Oval

One curved edge, like a
circle that's been squashed…

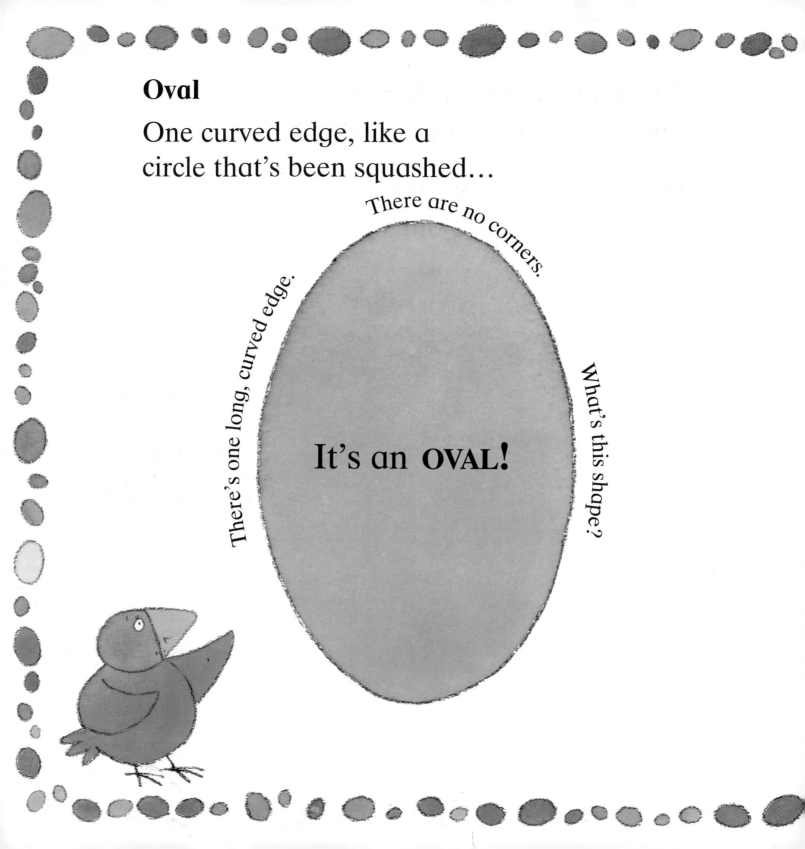

There are no corners.

There's one long, curved edge.

What's this shape?

It's an **OVAL!**

These eggs are oval shapes.
They are painted bright colours.

How many red eggs can you count?

I'd like a boiled egg for tea!

Diamond

Four straight sides, like a
square that's been squeezed...

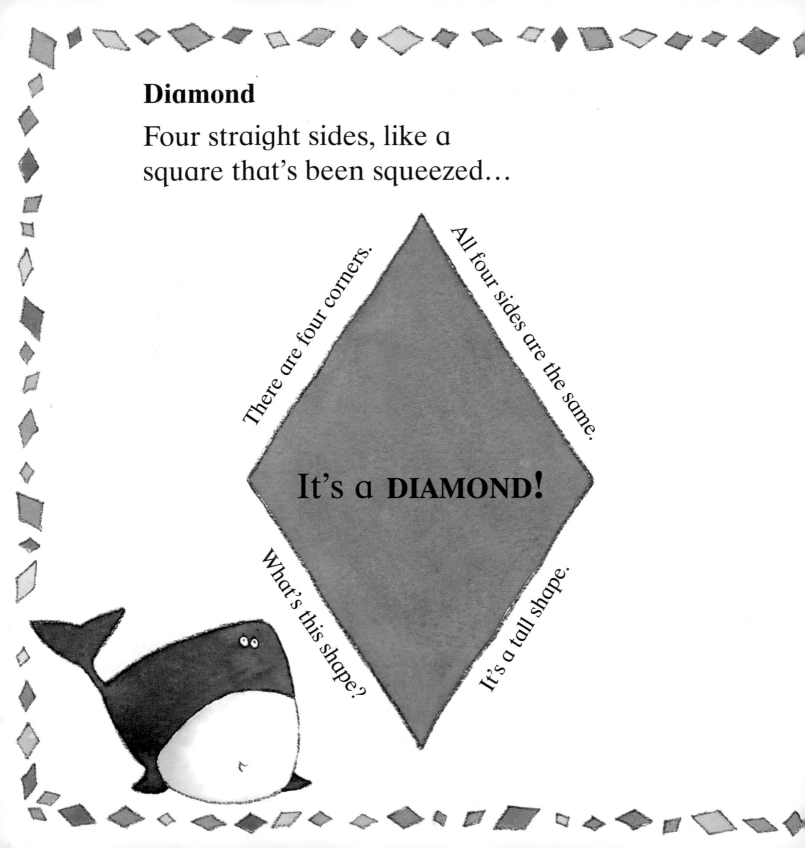

There are four corners.

All four sides are the same.

It's a **DIAMOND**!

What's this shape?

It's a tall shape.

These kites are diamond shapes.
Some are tall and some are wide.

Whose kite is yellow?

Colours and shapes

Here are all the colours and shapes together.

How many shapes can you name?
Which colours can you find?

Which is your favourite colour?
Which shape do you like best?